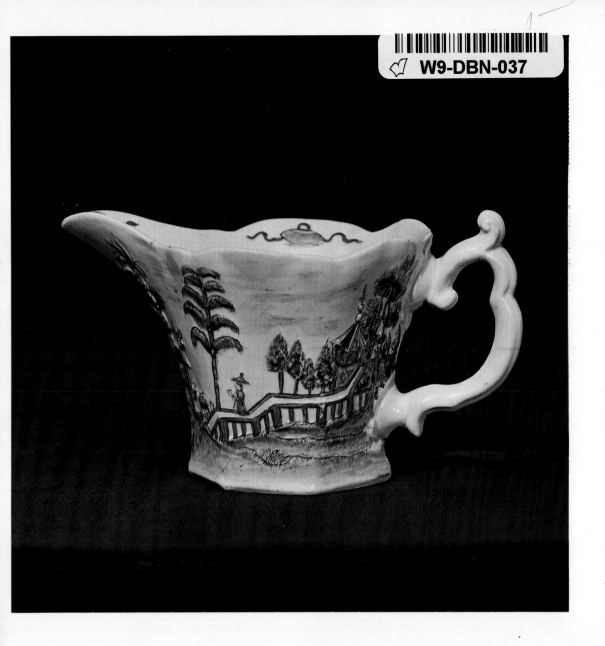

ROYAL WORCESTER

AND THE DYSON PERRINS MUSEUM

FRONT COVER: *Royal Worcester figurine of Queen Mary I (Mary Tudor), one of a series of six Queens Regnant of England, modelled by Ronald Van Ruyckevelt.*

BACK COVER: *A general view of part of the Dyson Perrins Museum of Royal Worcester Porcelain. It was opened by H.M. The Queen when Princess Elizabeth in 1951.*

ABOVE: *The famous Wigornia cream-boat, the first piece made by the Worcester Porcelain Company in 1751, marked under the base with the word* Wigornia, *the Latin name for the city of Worcester.*

ABOVE: *The First Period Factory. This engraving by Robert Hancock shows the Worcester Porcelain Manufactory in the late 1750s. The picture is evidence of the extensive alterations which had taken place since the first known representation of the factory buildings was published in 1752. The Severn offered a cheap and convenient way of bringing raw materials from Cornwall by ship like the one in the foreground.*

RIGHT: *Early Bristol/Worcester. These wares are among the first examples of porcelain to be made in the West of England. The central figure is marked BRISTOLL. The little butter-boat (right) was made at both Bristol and Worcester, and is known with either mark.*

FACING PAGE: *Dr. John Wall, M.D. (1708–76), was a Fellow of Merton College, Oxford, and a doctor in the city of Worcester who, among his many achievements, first popularized Malvern water. John Wall was a talented amateur painter of historical subjects, and his portrait which is in the Dyson Perrins Collection is reproduced here. He was one of the original shareholders in The Worcester Royal Porcelain Company formed in 1751.*

ROYAL WORCESTER

George Savage

THE Worcester Royal Porcelain Company is the oldest factory for the manufacture of porcelain in England today, first being established in 1751. It is one of the few enterprises where the traditional craftsmanship of the eighteenth century survives, and among its present-day wares the factory's craftsmen have produced porcelain of a quality undreamed of when it was founded.

Today, when porcelain tableware of excellent quality is both inexpensive and easy to buy, it is difficult for us to realize that the people of the eighteenth century regarded it as a rare and precious material. Porcelain was first imported from China, which is why it is often called 'china' today, and before 1700 it was wildly popular in fashionable circles. But even though the East Indiamen put into London with a hundred thousand pieces on board, the demand could not be supplied. Ingenious experimenters in the West sought eagerly for ways of making porcelain with varying success, and in England three factories were established within a few years of each other—at Bow and Chelsea in London, and at Bristol, the latter factory transferred to Worcester in 1751.

Bow and Chelsea have long since disappeared although, like Worcester, what they made then is eagerly sought by collectors. But Worcester survived to be the largest maker of fine china in England, with an international reputation which is second to none, and its eighteenth-century wares, when they appear in the great auction-rooms like Sotheby's and Christie's, bring prices which are often far higher than for those of the other factories of the time.

The factory's own collection of the wares of the past, which is the most comprehensive in existence today, is housed in the Dyson Perrins Museum, but nearly all of the world's great museums have important collections, notably the British Museum, the Victoria & Albert Museum, and the Ashmolean Museum at Oxford.

Today the Worcester factory makes bone-china, but in the eighteenth century its porcelain came very close to that of China. It is not surprising, therefore, that it first devoted its attention to wares in the Chinese style, even to the extent of calling itself the Worcester Tonquin Manufactory.

The Worcester story begins in Bristol with the grating of a licence to dig and search for soaprock near the Lizard, in Cornwall, to a Quaker manufacturer of brass and copper named Benjamin Lund. The use of soaprock was the key to the success of the new undertaking, and the Worcester factory did not relinquish this formula until bone-china was introduced early in the nineteenth century. Manufacture at Bristol began in 1749, and before the end of 1750 the factory was advertising for apprentices.

On the 4th June 1751, The Worcester Porcelain Company was formed to acquire the Bristol undertaking, and the Deed of Partnership, to which fifteen names were appended, still survives in the archives of the present Company.

The Company started with a

capital of £4,500, and the principal shareholders were William Baylies, Edward Cave, who edited the *Gentleman's Magazine*, and Richard Holdship, a Worcester glover. Smaller shares were taken by (among others) Josiah Holdship, maltster, Samuel Bradley, a goldsmith, Dr. John Wall (who was to give his name to the factory's early wares, which are often referred to as belonging to the 'Wall period'), and William Davis who, with Dr. Wall, was responsible for the transfer of the Bristol factory and its workmen to Worcester. Dr. Wall and Davies were given their shares of £250 apiece probably for the secret of manufacture, which they acquired from the earlier factory, and two workmen, Robert Podmore and John Lyes, were given a bonus for special services conditional on the new enterprise being

a profitable one. It is possible that these two men were key employees of the Bristol factory who brought the secret with them, for Podmore later defected and helped to start a factory in Liverpool, which made an inferior porcelain of the same kind as Worcester.

The old view that Dr. Wall actually invented the porcelain made at Worcester is incorrect, but undoubtedly he played a prominent part in perfecting it. It is probable that it never really left the experimental stage at Bristol, despite the remark of the eighteenth century traveller, Dr. Richard Pococke, who visited the factory and wrote: '. . . they make very beautiful white sauceboats adorned with reliefs of festoons, which sell for sixteen shillings a pair.'

There can be no doubt that in the

secret of making porcelain with soap-rock the new factory acquired an invaluable asset which enabled it to produce wares of very high quality from the first. To this fact the early wares in the Museum amply testify. English porcelain of the time made at either Bow or Chelsea, because it was extremely close to being a kind of glass, was prone to crack when boiling water was poured into it. Chinese porcelain, and the porcelain made at Worcester which closely resembled the Chinese ware in principle, did not suffer from this defect, a valuable advantage noticed at the time by Robert Dossie, author of *The Handmaid to the Arts*, a popular book of formulae used by craftsmen and manufacturers of the day which ran into several editions. Dossie wrote: 'A manufactory at Worcester has produced, even at very cheap prices, pieces that . . . bear hot water without more hazard than the true China ware.' In the *Annual Register* for 1763 we find: 'The Worcester [porcelain] has a good body, scarcely inferior to that coming from China; it is very tough and never scales off [i.e. never chips] . . . The tea-table, indeed, is completely furnished, and some Worcester porcelain is so well enamelled as to resemble the finest foreign wares.'

A great historian of the art of porcelain, and a very acute critic—the late R. L. Hobson of the British Museum—wrote in 1910: 'Another conspicuous virtue of the ware was neatness—neatness of form and neatness of finish so marked that by these two tests alone old Worcester can be distinguished from other English porcelain . . . Place a Worcester teapot beside a Bow teapot of the same style and compare the

*   *   *

LEFT: *A rare group of canaries on apple-blossom made by Worcester in about 1770.*

FACING PAGE (top): *Early coloured wares which, at the time when most factories were experiencing difficulty with this kind of decoration, gained for Worcester a well-deserved reputation for fine quality.*

FACING PAGE (below): *An interesting group of wares painted in the Oriental style, some with a palette very closely approaching that of China known as the famille rose. Contemporary Japanese styles are also known.*

fine proportions of one with the relative clumsiness of the other.'

Visitors to the Dyson Perrins Museum can try this test for themselves, and they will not, through the whole of Worcester's long history, find it to fail. The simple rounded forms thrown on the wheel, and the precision of the foot-rings with their sharp-cut sides, which characterize much of the service-ware, will be found in the wares of no other eighteenth-century English factory.

Among the partners Samuel Bradley was privileged to 'vend the ware when finished', and it has always been customary for goldsmiths to sell fine china, a tradition which still survives today. No doubt Bradley also influenced the forms of some of the early wares, which were based on those of contemporary silver.

By 1756 the factory had opened their first London wholesale warehouse 'for the better accommodation of merchants and traders' which was situated at London House, Aldersgate Street. Orders were taken there for the home and foreign trade, and it is probable that a considerable trade was being done with Holland at this time in blue painted porcelain in the Chinese manner, the Dutch also being the principal importers of this kind

       *   *   *

ABOVE LEFT: *Early Blue and White. Porcelain painted in blue underglaze was always popular at Worcester, much of it decorated in the fashionable Chinese style. The teapot was the only truly practical design of the time, and it is still popular today.*

LEFT: *The Invention of Printing. Transfer-printing was an innovation which helped to put decorated porcelain within the reach of more homes than had been able to afford hand-painted wares. Worcester remained the only porcelain factory to use printing on a commercial scale during the 18th century. The earliest quality printing was done on the surface of the glaze (centre), but Worcester soon perfected printing in underglaze blue (below).*

FACING PAGE: *The Tracy Mug. The painting of this mug resembles watercolour paintings by Dr. Wall in the Museum collection. The mug commemorates the election of Robert Tracy to Parliament in 1747.*

of porcelain from China. It is, indeed, possible—so close was the resemblance—that the Dutch were actually selling Worcester as Chinese porcelain, which the appearance of pseudo-Chinese marks on some Worcester porcelain makes more likely. There could be no greater testimony than this to the quality of the ware.

The first fairly complete picture of Worcester in the eighteenth century has been left to us by Valentine Green, an engraver who had worked at the factory. In his *Survey of the City of Worcester* published in 1764 he begins by giving the location of the factory—'. . . in Mardyke near the Severn, having it on the west, Warmstreyslip on the north, St. Alban's Church and Fish Street on the east, and the Bishop's palace and the cathedral on the south. It was originally a large mansion-house [known as Warmstry House] which, with its adjacent offices, is converted to a pleasing scene of art and industry.' He describes the various departments of manufacture, including a room where the ware was turned on a lathe, which is one of the secrets of Worcester precision and neatness. He describes also a large iron rowl, 'upwards of two tons in weight', powered by two horses, which reduced the material used in the preparation of the body to a fine powder.

The earliest Worcester porcelain was painted in blue under the glaze, and this continued to be the most popular ware throughout the first ten years of the factory's life. The more difficult art of painting on the glaze in enamel colours was mastered, but such wares formed a much smaller part of the early production, although the examples which have survived are of unusually high quality, delicately painted in a linear style. Like the blue-painted wares, Chinese subjects are the rule.

Worcester even then, at a time when they found it almost essential to copy and adapt Chinese designs to survive, showed an unusual responsiveness to new ideas, and the factory was the first to produce porcelain decorated with transfer-prints on a large scale. Valentine Green refers to the process, saying 'The curious and valuable art of transferring prints on porcelain is, in this factory, arrived at and carried

on in the greatest perfection. The work is the employ and subsistence of a great number of people.'

Transfer-printing is a peculiarly English technique, and has been employed only to a very limited extent on the Continent. An engraved copper-plate was inked with ceramic colour and a print taken from it on to paper. While the ink was still tacky the paper was pressed on to the porcelain surface, leaving behind an impression of the design in monochrome. Most prints are on the glaze in black, or in one or two simple colours such as purple and brick-red, but some are in blue applied to the ware before glazing. Transfer-prints on old Worcester porcelain are of two kinds—the most common has all the hatchings and shadings of an engraving, and is complete in itself. The second variety is an outline only, and the outline was later filled in with enamel colours by semi-skilled workmen. The second type was introduced by Worcester as an aid to quantity production before 1760, and it was not until 1770 that the enterprising Josiah Wedgwood suggested introducing this method to his partner, Bentley, saying 'I do not think any . . . . of the Painters you will employ ought to, or will object to the assistance of an outline, especially if to the most delicate ones it is offered rather upon the idea of *dispatch* so necessary in a manufacture . . .'

The actual origin of the process is controversial, and there are several contenders for the honour of having discovered it, but the man who first applied it to the decoration of porcelain was the Birmingham engraver, Robert Hancock. Examples of his work are to be found on Battersea enamel, and on some primitively printed specimens of Bow porcelain, but by about 1756 Hancock had arrived at Worcester, and although his earliest prints are a little blurred, the technique had soon been mastered. The process of printing in black became known as 'jet enamelling', and some of the best examples are found among the well-known famous portraits of Frederick the Great, the King of Prussia, who was England's ally in the Seven Years War, which are dated 1757. Among the other engravers who worked at Worcester, the names of Valentine Green (from whom we have quoted), James Ross, and John

Lowick are known. Thomas Turner, who later made porcelain at the Caughley factory to imitate Worcester, may have been one of them.

These very pleasant wares, so characteristic of early Worcester production, are today eagerly sought by collectors, and exist in considerable variety.

By the 1760s new fashions and new ideas in art and decoration were beginning to emerge in England. The Adam Brothers were starting to popularize the strictly classical style associated with their name, and Chinese subjects were falling rapidly out of favour. The Chelsea factory had been copying the sumptuous decorations of the royal porcelain factory at Sèvres since 1758. Sèvres, owned by Louis Quinze, was able to employ the greatest artists of the time as designers (François Boucher was one of them), and the most skilled craftsmen to execute their designs. The designs of Adam were much more suited to pottery than to porcelain, a fact of which the rising Josiah Wedgwood was not slow to take advantage.

It might be thought that an English Midlands factory, separated from the Metropolis by the almost impassable roads of the time, had small chance of adapting itself to a changing scene of this kind, where the choice lay between a form and a type of decoration entirely unsuited

to the porcelain medium, or of competing with a factory in so powerful a position as that of Sèvres.

Nevertheless Worcester thrived on difficulties, and in this decade—between 1760 and 1770—it blossomed forth with rich ground colours and elaborate painting of a quality worthy to stand beside much of the production of its French rival, and it became the only European factory to do comparable work. Only perhaps in the sheer beauty of the French porcelain body was Worcester at a disadvantage, but this was eventually to prove a fatal handicap to Sèvres, since it was so difficult and expensive to make that they were forced to abandon it, and in 1774 they, too, began to adopt a close approximation to the Chinese porcelain body. After this year *vieux Sèvres*, porcelain of the eighteenth century aristocracy and nineteenth century millionaires, was made only for special purposes, and it was discontinued entirely at the Revolution of 1793.

Naturally so drastic a change, which

meant not only increasing the output of fine quality enamelled wares but a progressive abandonment of Oriental *motifs* in favour of purely European patterns, took time to organize. Although painting in enamels on the glaze had been undertaken by the Worcester factory almost from the first, skilled enamellers were always rare, and the early English porcelain factories had to look for their craftsmen to such trades as the fan-painters of London and Birmingham.

All the factories of the day also put out a great deal of work to independent decorators, to whom they sent white porcelain to be painted in colours. The names of several are known, all working in London, and the most notable of them in 1760 was James Giles of Clerkenwell who decorated Bow, Chelsea, Worcester and Chinese porcelain.

Some of the fine quality painting on Worcester porcelain in the 1760s was undoubtedly done by Giles, and he was provided by the factory with porcelain ready-decorated with the famous scale-blue ground, to which

he added panels of colourful birds and flowers framed with elaborate gilding. One type of bird in particular (known to collectors as 'dishevelled birds' from the somewhat untidy appearance of the plumage) has certainly been identified as the work of Giles, and sliced fruit painting undoubtedly came from the same source.

The nature of Giles's connection with the factory is obscure but in 1767 Worcester advertised 'an enamelling branch in London', which is seemingly a reference to him, and Giles's account-books record his purchases of porcelain from 'William Davis & Co.' of Worcester, which suggests that Davis had taken charge of this aspect of the Company's business.

In 1768 the situation seems to have altered considerably. Due to the illness of its proprietor, the Chelsea factory was now moribund, and some of its skilled painters, well accustomed to the richness of contemporary Sèvres styles, evidently migrated to Worcester, because in this year the

Scale Blue and Coloured Grounds

Blue grounds produced from cobalt oxide, with oriental or European style decorations in reserved panels, are the most famous colours produced by Worcester, who were able to control this very difficult effect superbly. The blue grounds *(facing page)* were often painted with beautiful scales, which shimmer under the surface. The other ground colours (green, yellow, claret and pink scale are shown above) were copies of Meissen and Sèvres and typical of the workmanship are the paintings of the 'fabulous' birds on the green ground vase and the hand piercing on the yellow ground basket.

Scale Blue Mask Jug

Mask jugs, sometimes modelled with overlapping cabbage leaves as the body and with a man's face on the front as a spout are one of the most typical shapes produced by Worcester. First made during the Dr. Wall period they have continued in manufacture to the present day. In the 18th century the mask jug was called the 'Dutch' jug, possibly a reference to the fact that it resembled a well-known jug, which had a caricature of Cardinal Bellamine on the spout. The mask jug illustrated here was made in about 1776, the year of Dr. Wall's death.

9

LEFT: *A superb pair of larger cider mugs with a capacity for 4¼ pints each made for the Marquis of Abergavenny, signed and painted with figure subjects by Humphrey Chamberlain and coats of arms. When painted in 1813 the original cost was £42, a considerable sum in those days.*

★

FACING PAGE: *Probably the most impressive piece made by Chamberlain of Worcester, this magnificent large vase and cover made in about 1820 celebrates the glorious victory at Waterloo. The painting shows the famous meeting of the Duke of Wellington and Marshall Blucher, commander of the Prussian army, on the battlefield at dusk on 18 June 1815.*

★

BELOW: *A set of Chamberlain's Worcester figures of the Rainer family, who came from the Tyrol Valley to sing and dance in London in 1826 and 1827. The set of 'Tyrolese' cost £2 in the 1826 order books.*

factory advertised that they had 'engaged the best painters from Chelsea', and that 'any orders will be executed in the highest taste and much cheaper than can be afforded by any Painters in London'.

Decorators like Giles, who did not make porcelain but who enamelled the productions of the great factories, are usually termed 'outside decorators' in England. They were rather more numerous on the Continent, where the work of the most competent is very highly valued. The best of the English decorators are no less valued here, and one whose work is much finer than that generally attributed to the Giles studio is Jeffreys Hamet O'Neale, an Irish miniaturist, who first made his appearance as a porcelain painter at Chelsea in 1752. It is possible that he left Chelsea to work near or with James Giles, and he was elected to membership of the Society of Artists in 1765. Between 1768 and 1770 he may have lived at Worcester, although there is no definite evidence to confirm the supposition. It is, however, tempting to think that he executed his magnificent vase-painting in the City. He is represented in the Dyson Perrins Museum by some remarkable fine examples of his work.

He was closely rivalled by a Scottish miniaturist, John Donaldson, who worked in London but who was probably employed directly by the factory. Both O'Neale and Donaldson signed their work, a privilege extended in the eighteenth century only to the most valued artists.

Some bird-painting of exceptional quality done about 1775, and very much in the style of exotic birds painted at Sèvres about 1760, have been attributed to Fidelé Duvivier, a French-born Chelsea painter (who probably also worked for Giles and may have been employed at Worcester), or to a certain 'M. Soqui', said to have been a painter from Sèvres, who at one time worked in the small Plymouth factory started by William Cookworthy in 1768.

Although many coloured grounds were used decoratively during the period from 1760 to 1780—deep blue, apple green, yellow, claret (a version of the *rose Pompadour* of Sèvres), and turquoise—the most widely known are the 'scale blues', a ground formed of a pattern of overlapping scales in blue. The origin of this pattern is not known, but it occurs on sixteenth-century Italian *maiolica*, and a variation of it became popular in Germany under the name of *mosaik* in the early 1760s. Scale-blue is an underglaze ground; scale-patterns in enamel colours on the glaze were probably the work of Giles.

One of the most dramatic discoveries of recent years has been the identification of eighteenth century Worcester figures. At one time some collectors thought that nothing of this kind was made at Worcester, despite a reference in the *Public Advertiser* of 1769 to 'Jars, Beakers, and figures', and the diary of Mrs. Philip Lybbe Powys who, in 1771, described a visit to the factory in her diary. She wrote afterwards '. . . in this room they make the china ornaments and figures; these are done in moulds, separate moulds for the limbs, and stuck on . . .', which describes the process very well. Other collectors searched for Worcester figures without knowing exactly what they looked like. At first a group of

Eighteenth-century porcelain

ABOVE: This beautiful plate, formed of raised rose leaves and rose buds, is known as the 'Blind Earl' pattern. First produced by Worcester in about 1760 (the one illustrated is of this date) it has continued to be made at most periods since and is still in production today. The original 'Blind Earl' was the Earl of Coventry, a great lover of porcelain, who lost his sight as a result of a hunting accident. No longer able to see, he ordered a pattern from Worcester that he could feel. An early form of Braille in porcelain.

FACING PAGE (above and below): Donaldson and O'Neale Vases. The wealthy 18th-century collectors of fine porcelain especially loved groups of vases, termed garnitures, which would decorate a chimney-piece or stand on a side-table. They could be in groups of three or five, and sometimes even seven, contrasting shapes. The garnitures shown here are among the finest

produced by Worcester and are some of the finest items in the Dyson Perrins Museum. Both groups have superb underglaze cobalt blue grounds and gilding and were made about 1770. The painter of the garniture above right was John Donaldson, a Scotsman, and the scenes are based upon the paintings of Boucher. The group below right were painted by J. H. O'Neale, an Irishman, and are of classical or fable subjects. All six vases have a blue fretted square mark on the base, the normal mark to be found on Worcester Porcelain of this period, with cobalt blue ground and on-glaze enamel paintings.

★

RIGHT: Royal Worcester Porcelain Marks. Worcester factory marks of the Dr. Wall period were the crescent and script W on underglaze blue pieces and the fretted square on richer blue grounds. The present trade mark uses the cresent and four Ws plus the crown and '51', an abbreviation for 1751, the year of foundation.

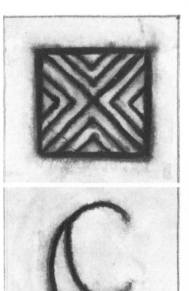

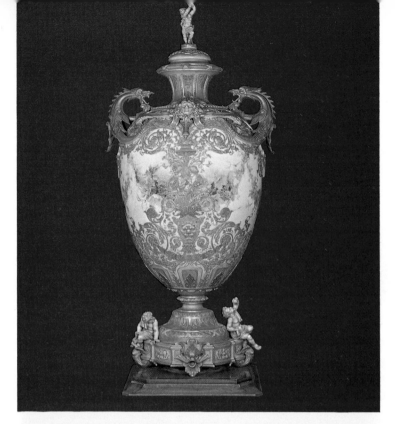

ABOVE (left): *The magnificent Chicago Exhibition vase, modelled by James Hadley for the exhibition of 1893. Its height is 4′ 6″; it is the largest piece of porcelain made by Worcester and it took a year to produce.*

*

ABOVE (right): *A beautiful study of a veiled lady, modelled by James Hadley, and glazed with a soft 'ivory' effect typical of the 1860s.*

*

LEFT: *A superb large Worcester vase, made during the Flight and Barr period in about 1815, painted by Thomas Baxter with a view of Carisbroke Castle. The quality of painting and gilding was equal to anything in the whole of Europe.*

*

FACING PAGE: *An incredible vase and cover pierced by eye and hand alone by George Owen in 1893. George was the greatest exponent in the world of the difficult craft of piercing clay while it was still in the wet stage.*

14

figures bearing the Worcester crescent mark were favoured candidates for the honour of having been made here, but these proved to have come from Bow, painted by Giles, and since Giles was painting a good deal of Worcester porcelain at the time, quite probably the crescent was added on his instructions. But Hobson shrewdly remarked that no one forges the signature of a man without a banking account, and the existence of such figures strongly suggested that those from Worcester remained to be found. They were finally identified by the late William King of the British Museum in 1923, and his judgement was confirmed by chemical analysis.

As soon as the first examples were known, others began to be identified. They all seemed to bear marked resemblances in style of modelling to certain figures from Bow, and some have the impressed mark $T°$ associated with a modeller there known as 'Mr. Tebo'—probably a Frenchman whose name was originally Thibaud. These were all made about 1770, when Tebo must have been employed by the factory. His work has now been traced at several English factories, although the only written record of him is to be found in the letters of Josiah Wedgwood.

Several different models have now been recorded, although specimens are exceedingly rare and very highly valued. Today the Worcester Royal Porcelain Company is world-famous for its figures, some of which, although they are not nearly so rare, are so fine in quality that they have commanded even higher prices in the world's auction-rooms than those of the eighteenth century.

Dr. Wall died in 1776, and the factory was directed by William Davis until his own death in 1783. It was then bought by the London agent, Thomas Flight, who intended it for his sons. In 1793 Martin Barr, a man of considerable technical ability, was taken into partnership, and a number of changes in the organisation took place, then and later. Successively the style was Flight (1783–1793), Flight & Barr (1793–1807), Barr, Flight & Barr (1807–1813), and Flight, Barr & Barr (1813–1840). The porcelain of the Flight period, which ended in 1793, was usually simple in form and decoration, much of it painted with small floral sprays, often inspired by those devised for Marie-Antoinette by her own Paris factory which became almost equally popular in England.

In August, 1788, the factory was honoured by a visit from George III and Queen Charlotte, the first of many royal visits during its lifetime, when Worcester received permission to describe itself as 'Manufacturers to their Majesties'. The King chose a pattern called the 'Blue Lily', which was renamed the 'Royal Lily', and this is still extremely popular. At this time Worcester began to adopt the new fashion for topographical painting on porcelain, which included many local views. Especially after 1790 the factory employed an increasing number of talented artists, including John (or James) Pennington, Thomas Baxter, probably William Billingsley (later founder of the short-lived Nantgarw factory), Robert Brewer, and Moses Webster.

In 1783, when the factory was sold to Flight, Robert Chamberlain (who probably directed the enamelling studios) left to found a studio of his own in King Street, Worcester, painting white porcelain bought from Caughley. About 1792 he started his own factory for the manufacture of porcelain on the site of the present factory. His early wares were undistinguished, and resemble the minor contemporary wares of Flight & Barr. They received at least two important commissions however, one for a service for Lord Nelson in 1802 and the other for a service for the Duke of Cumberland in 1806. In 1811 Chamberlain's introduced their 'Regent' body, named in honour of the Prince of Wales to whom they had already been appointed manu-

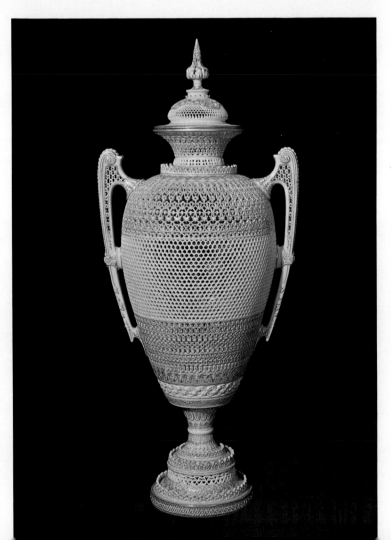

facturers, who became Regent in this year. 'Regent' porcelain was of exceptional quality, very expensive to produce, and only used for special orders. As an example we may take a service produced in 1816 for the ill-fated Princess Charlotte which then cost £1,050 or one for the East India Company of Madras which then cost £4,190.

By 1833 trading conditions were becoming difficult, partly because of prevailing economic conditions which led eventually to the 'hungry forties', and partly because of competition from inferior wares, such as the so-called 'stone china' made in Staffordshire, and the two Worcester enterprises agreed to amalgamate. Flight, Barr & Barr moved to the Chamberlain factory, where new buildings were constructed, and the old site is now a Technical College. The present factory stands on Chamberlain's site.

For a time, so bad were conditions generally, that the factory was forced largely to concentrate on wares of purely domestic utility, and the more decorative wares for which the factory had achieved so great a reputation were discontinued until after the Great Exhibition of 1851. In 1852 one of the directors, W. H. Kerr, formed a new Company, in

which he was joined by R. W. Binns.

Both Kerr and Binns were men of taste who presided over a revival of the ornamental wares which had made the earlier factories famous. Biscuit porcelain—porcelain without a glaze—which had been devised and popularized by the Sèvres factory in the eighteenth century had already been revived in Staffordshire and renamed 'Parian' ware or 'Statuary Porcelain', and this was employed very successfully in a famous Worcester service depicting scenes from Shakespeare's *A Midsummer Night's Dream*, with figure-modelling by Kirk. Notable work inspired by the enamel-painting of Limoges was done by Thomas Bott (and his son Thomas John Bott) at the suggestion of the Prince-Consort, and painting of high quality appears on a service done in 1863 for the marriage of the Prince of Wales (later H.M. King Edward VII) and Princess Alexandra. A richly-decorated service made for the marriage of the Earl and Countess of Dudley revived the jewelled decoration of Sèvres, reputedly invented by Cotteau in 1781, in which precious stones were simulated by drops of translucent enamel.

The enterprise became a limited company in 1862 under the guidance

of R. W. Binns, when it was styled The Worcester Royal Porcelain Company in recognition of the many

*   *   *

ABOVE: *The Nelson Service. Lord Nelson, accompanied by Lady Hamilton, visited Chamberlain in 1802 and ordered a variety of porcelain. Only a breakfast-service was finished, and a specimen is shown here.*

FACING PAGE (above left): *The quality of decorative vases at the turn of the 18th century was due to the rise of a new school of porcelain painting, and an improved method of gilding. In form, this Flight vase is characteristic of the many produced at this time.*

FACING PAGE (above right): *From about 1855 to 1885 James and Thomas Callowhill were among the most noted Worcester artists, especially for figure subjects, and Thomas Bott (1829–70) was famous for this work in the style of old French enamels from Limoges. This vase was the joint work of Callowhill and Bott.*

FACING PAGE (below): *The Dudley Service. It was made for presentation to the Countess of Dudley in 1865. The gilding and jewelled work was by Samuel Ranford, and the panels of female heads by Thomas Callowhill.*

ABOVE: *Some of Owen's pierced porcelain* (left) *required an almost superhuman degree of skill and many weeks of patient efforts to complete. Owen was perhaps inspired by the intricacy of Oriental ivory carving. Wares in the Japanese style* (right) *introduced by Binns, enjoyed great popularity. The porcelain, ivory in tone, is enhanced with differently coloured gilding and bronzing. Introduced in 1872, Japanese pieces were exhibited at Vienna in 1873, and some of the more elaborate were modelled by Hadley and decorated by Callowhill and the gilder Bejot.*

LEFT: *Harry Davis and Stinton Vases. Royal Worcester artists are noted for long service. The central vase was painted by Harry Davis, who started with the factory in 1898 and who was only recently retired. He painted many of the factory's most important 20th-century commissions. The Highland cattle-scenes are by John Stinton, an especially noted painter of this popular subject, who was born in 1854 and died in 1956.*

FACING PAGE: *This nautilus shell cup by Hadley and Callowhill was exhibited at the Paris Exposition of 1878. It is based on the shells superbly mounted ·in the 16th century by the Augsburg goldsmiths, much sought by collectors of the time.*

occasions on which it had been awarded royal patronage. During the second half of the nineteenth century it assumed the lead in the manufacture of ornamental porcelain which it has maintained ever since, introducing many new techniques eagerly copied elsewhere. Among them was porcelain inspired by the art of Japan which was then enjoying great popularity in the West. In 1872 a decoration of bronze and differently coloured gilding on an ivory porcelain was introduced, most of it decorated in the Japanese taste, which was highly praised by the *Art Journal*, and especially commended when it was exhibited in Vienna in 1873. At the Paris Exhibition of 1878 Worcester was not only awarded a Gold Medal for its products, but R. W. Binns was granted the Cross of the Legion of Honour.

From 1875 onwards ornamental modelling of very high quality was done by the talented James Hadley (noted for 'Grecian' figures), and his three sons. Most notable is his pair of vases in a revived Renaissance style depicting potters at work, of which two pairs exist, one being in the United States. The Hadleys later started a small factory of their own in Bath Road, Worcester, which was purchased by the Worcester Royal Porcelain Company after James Hadley's death in 1903, the sons and their staff returning to the parent company in 1905.

A small factory had been founded at Worcester in 1801 by Thomas Grainger which began by copying the wares of Flight and Chamberlain. They also manufactured ornamental ware in Parian porcelain, and an interesting development was the 'bower' group of figures surrounded by an overarching 'bower' of delicately modelled flowers, foreshadowing those later developed by Dorothy Doughty to accompany her superb bird-models in modern times. Both Grainger and Chamberlain made pierced or reticulated porcelain first made by the Chinese in the Ming dynasty which was later perfected at the Royal Porcelain Works by George Owen. These vases made by Owen, much sought by collectors today, exhibit almost superhuman skill, and some of the older craftsmen at the factory still remember him working on them. He died in 1917 at a very advanced age.

The Royal Porcelain Works entered the twentieth century as a prosperous and flourishing concern which had already developed a tradition of fostering and encouraging individual craftsmen and designers, and this enlightened policy has been its greatest strength, giving its products an individuality and quality which has set them apart from those of its competitors. 'Royal Worcester' in porcelain is now a synonym for superlative quality. But the twentieth century also brought many changes in demand, with which the factory has kept pace—from 1912 to 1953 under the guidance of Charles William Dyson Perrins, born in 1864, who became Mayor of Worcester in 1897 and High Sheriff of the County in 1899. He achieved fame as a collector of medieval illuminated manuscripts and of early Worcester porcelain, and his collection of Worcester porcelain forms the major part of the exhibits in the Museum.

During his chairmanship many services were made for royalty in every part of the world, especially Japan and India. A particularly rich service was made in 1926 for H.H. the Maharajah Jam Sahib of Nawanagar, affectionately known to generations of cricket-lovers as 'Ranji'. This was decorated by Harry Davis, with views of the Maharajah's Indian palaces and notable English views, including his gardens at Staines and specimens are in the Museum. The most historic piece to be painted by Harry Davis was the vase made for presentation to Sir Winston Churchill which has an eighteenth century view of Worcester Cathedral.

Superb table services are still produced, often to special order and pattern, some of the most spectacular of recent years being made for the Middle East. Perhaps the most lovely service of all was a dessert set made at the request of the members of the Royal Household for presentation to Her Majesty The Queen to commemorate her Silver Jubilee. This was hand-painted with scenes of the royal pets such as the corgis, sporting dogs and horses.

Dorothy Doughty Birds

Dorothy Doughty was one of the greatest modellers in porcelain of our time. Her famous series of American and British birds now form collectors' pieces on both sides of the Atlantic Since the art of porcelain making became known in Europe 250 years ago, no ceramic modeller's work has enjoyed such popularity in their own lifetime. The quality of her work guarantees it a place among the fabulous antiques of the future.

'White Doves' by Van Ruyckevelt

To commemorate the Silver Wedding of H.M. The Queen and H.R.H. The Duke of Edinburgh, Royal Worcester commissioned from sculptor Ronald Van Ruyckevelt a special model which was to be limited to 25 copies. With such a small edition, it was not easy to determine a subject or a composition which would have a related Silver Wedding connotation, but Van Ruyckevelt's eventual sculpture simply called 'White Doves' captures the spirit of the occasion. The fine bone chine model itself is $17\frac{1}{2}''$ high and is mounted on an $8\frac{1}{2}''$ high plinth.